GUY'S GUIDES

You Ought to Know

A Guy's Guide to Sex

Bill Kelly

the rosen publishing group's
rosen central
new york

I would like to thank Elizabeth Frankenberger for generously putting me in touch with Rosen Publishing, and my editor at Rosen, Erica Smith, for her enthusiasm and guidance.

Published in 2000 by The Rosen Publishing Group, Inc.
29 East 21st Street, New York, NY 10010

Kelly, Bill.
        You oughta know : a guy's guide to sex / Bill Kelly.
                p. cm. — (Guys' guides)
        Includes bibliographical references and index.
    Summary: This book explains the physical and emotional changes a guy experiences during puberty.
        ISBN 0-8239-3084-X
    1. Puberty—Juvenile literature. 2. Sex instruction for boys—Juvenile literature. 3. Puberty—Juvenile literature. 4. Teenage boys—Sexual behavior—Juvenile literature. [1. Puberty. 2. Sex instruction for boys.] I. Title. II. Series.
613.9'53—dc21

<<< About This Book >>>

>>> Contents >>>

>> About this book <<

It's not easy being a guy these days. You're expected to be buff, studly, and masculine, but at the same time, you're supposed to be sensitive, thoughtful, and un-macho. And that's not all. You have to juggle all of this while you're wading through the shark-infested waters of middle school. So not only are you dealing with raging hormones, cliques, and geeks, and body changes, but you're also supposed to figure out how to be a Good Guy. As if anyone is even sure what that means anyway. It's enough to make you wish for the caveman days, when guys just grunted and wrestled mammoths with their bare hands and stuff.

Being an adolescent is complicated. Take girls, for example. Just five minutes ago—or so it seems—they weren't much different from you and your buddies. Now, suddenly you can't keep your eyes off them, and other parts of your body have taken an interest too. Or maybe you're not interested in girls yet, and you're worried about when you will be. Then there's figuring out where you fit into the middle school world. Are you a jock, a brain, or what? And how come it seems that someone else gets to decide for you? What's up with that?

Yeah, it's tough. Still, you're a smart guy, and you'll figure it all out. That's not to say that we can't all use a hand. That's where this book comes in. It's sort of a cheat sheet for all the big tests that your middle school years throw at you. Use it to help you get through the amazing maze of your life—and to come out alive on the other side.

<<< A Change Will Do You Good >>>

1

You may not know exactly when it happened. You didn't see a big sign in the road . . .

But sometime not so long ago, somewhere along the way, something changed. Maybe you were playing a game of touch football when you realized you stank to the high heavens. Maybe you grew six inches in six months. Maybe hairs started sprouting out of your body in places where they never did before. And then you put two and two together and thought "four!" (Just kidding.) You thought "puberty," and here you are, reading this book. Congratulations.

Welcome to Puberty
Population: You

Or maybe nothing's happening yet, but you know something big is on the way. You want to be prepared. Good for you.

Now let's get down to business.

>> Why Is This Happening to Me? <<

All of the changes your body is going through now—or is about to go through—are being caused by chemicals called hormones.

When your body reaches a certain age (for guys it's usually between nine and twelve), your body releases hormones to trigger puberty. Boys and girls both have these hormones but in differing amounts. The hormones work in different ways in different places in girls and boys.

Depending on your age, you may have already started to notice some changes when you look in the mirror or go through your day. So here's a rundown of what to expect. Most of this should happen by the time you're in your late teens, but everyone is different. Don't worry if you seem to be lagging behind. You'll get there soon enough. We all do.

>> Face-Off <<

During puberty, acne, or pimples, pretty much comes with the territory. All those hormones running around your body can throw off the balance of oils in your skin and cause zits. Some days it can be so bad that you want to change faces with somebody else, but most people have just a few annoying pimples here or there. Some people decide to go to a skin doctor, or dermatologist, if their acne is really bad. But in general, all you can do is keep your skin clean, hope you don't have a huge zit on your nose the day class pictures are taken, and wait it out.

Oh yeah, and don't pick or squeeze or pop. It could cause scarring. And remember this: Objects in your own mirror always seem bigger than they really are. You may think you've got a zit the size of Mount Everest, but a lot of people aren't even going to notice it.

>> Big Time <<

You will probably go through some growth spurts during puberty. These are short periods of time during which you grow a lot, like four or more inches in a year. It's possible you'll be changing the sizes of your

jeans and shoes faster than you can break them in. To keep up, you're probably going to start eating more to give your growing body the energy it needs.

As you grow taller, you'll also change shape. Your shoulders will widen, and you'll become more muscular. If your breasts start to grow, don't panic; you're not suddenly turning into a woman. Any slight enlargement of the breasts should go away shortly.

>> How Do You Like Them Apples? <<

During puberty, your voice will change. Until it settles in, this can be kind of embarrassing because your voice will crack and do all sorts of funny things when you least want it to, such as when you're reading aloud in class or talking to a cute girl. During this time, your voice box, or larynx, will grow, and you'll develop a bulge, or Adam's apple, on the front of your neck.

>> Hair We Are! <<

Once your voice has changed, you'll probably start growing facial hair. You probably won't be able to grow a full lumberjack-style beard for years—if ever. Most likely you'll start out with pretty light growth, which will get heavier as you get older. Depending on how much facial hair you have, you'll have to start shaving sooner or later.

You'll also start to grow hair around your penis and testicles—this is called pubic hair—along with hair on your chest and under your arms. How much hair you'll have in all of these places depends on genes you've inherited from your family. Some men, for example, will have tons of chest hair, whereas others will reach adulthood and still have smooth, hairless chests. There's not much you can do about it either way, so just wait and see what develops.

before

after

>> Smells Like Teen Spirit (or "Putting the P.U. in Puberty") <<

There's one more not-so-fun side effect of all those hormones. This is when your own body odor kicks in. You're probably going to stink if you work up too much of a sweat.

If you haven't already started showering daily, this is the time to start. It's also time to start wearing deodorant or antiperspirant.

So is that it?

Well, no. But you knew that already, didn't you? Because we've barely mentioned . . . drumroll, please . . . your penis.

There. We said it. Penis. And we're going to say it again. Penis. And again. Penis. In fact, we're going to dedicate a whole chapter to it . . .

2

<<< What's Up Down There? >>>

If you think about it, the whole penis thing is pretty weird. It's this hypersensitive organ—sometimes that's good and sometimes that's bad—and it's right smack between your legs on the outside of your body. We've got to wear a protective cup or jockstrap to protect it during contact sports. We completely flip out if anyone even jokes about kicking us anywhere near it. And strangest of all, we use it not just to urinate, but eventually to have sex! It's no wonder so many guys give their penises pet names.

>> Does Size Matter? <<

As you go through puberty, your penis will grow in size. Your testicles, too, will get bigger and hang lower than before. A lot of guys become obsessed with their penis size, which is understandable. It's also kind of point-

less because you can't do much about it anyway. It's important to remember that everyone develops at different rates and that every penis is as unique as the guy carrying it around. Most guys fall between 3 1/4 inches and 4 1/4 inches when soft and 5 and 8 inches when hard. Six is about average. The size of your penis doesn't affect your ability to enjoy sex and to enter into good sexual relationships.

True or False?

If one of my testicles hangs lower than the other, I'm a deformed freak.

False: It's entirely normal—actually, it's pretty common—for one testicle to hang lower than the other.

Circum . . . what?

Many parents have boys circumcised when they're infants. This means that the foreskin, a layer of skin that surrounds the shaft of the penis, is cut away by a doctor. (They probably do this when we're babies so that we can't sit up and scream, "No way are you getting anywhere near me with a knife!")

An uncircumcised penis will have a tube of skin that drops down over the tip when soft. It retracts, or pulls back, to expose the head of the penis when you have an erection. If you've been circumcised, the layer has been cut away and you can see the tip of your penis at all times.

There are a lot of different opinions on circumcision, but all you really need to know right now is that it doesn't make a difference in your ability to have—and enjoy—sex later in life. If you're curious, you can ask your parents why you were or weren't circumcised.

>> It's Part of My Body, So Why Does It Have a Mind of Its Own? <<

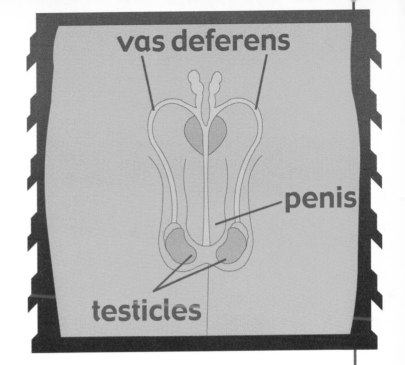

If you haven't already figured this out, you will soon: Your penis and your brain do not always see eye-to-eye. Right now, your body is preparing for adolescence and adulthood, during which you will become sexually active. So in order to make sure that everything is up and running before it sends you out into the adult world, your body has a few ways of testing things out; they're like trial runs to make sure all your equipment is working smoothly. Because of this, you may often feel that your penis has a mind of its own.

> I haven't wet my bed since I was a little kid. What's the deal? <

If you wake up and feel a wet spot in your bed, don't freak out. You haven't lost control of your bladder. You've had a

wet dream. (Technically, they're called nocturnal emissions, which you have to admit sounds more like a zookeeper's term for bat farts.) Wet dreams are totally normal, and every guy has them. They're test runs for the process of ejaculation, a crucial part of sex.

Here's what's happening: Inside your testicles, the hormone testosterone has triggered the production of sperm—tiny cells with tails that are able to fertilize a woman's egg during sex in order to make a baby. The sperm then travel through many windy little tubes, as well as through the larger tubes called the vas deferens. When your body is stimulated in certain ways—like during sex—a series of muscle contractions will pump sperm out of your penis in a fluid called semen.

Still with me?

Okay. During the night, your penis alternates between flaccid (soft) and erect (hard), depending on blood flow to that area. In fact, as you get older you may notice that you often wake up with an erection. And during puberty, because your body is testing itself out, you will not only have erections during your sleep, but you will also ejaculate, or release semen. So the sticky liquid on your sheets is not urine. Actually, when you have an erection, a valve closes off the path from your bladder so that urine cannot come out of the penis during sex.

You don't have to worry about ejaculating without warning when you're awake. It will normally take more stimuli (like touching or sexual contact of some kind) to make that happen. And although you can't always count on your penis to behave while you're snoozing these days, you can sleep easy knowing you won't have wet dreams all your life. They'll stop before puberty is over.

What's Up, Doc?

When you enter puberty and you have a checkup, the doctor might lightly cup your testicles and ask you to cough. He or she isn't a pervert! Your doctor is checking to make sure that your testes are actually inside the scrotum. Sometimes they don't drop down properly. He or she is also checking for any other abnormalities.

And if you ever get an erection in the doctor's office? As hard as it may be (ha ha), really, really, really try not to be embarrassed. Doctors are used to it. It's nothing they haven't seen before. Really.

> While I'm sleeping is one thing, but can't this thing behave during school? <

You may already have had the embarrassing experience of getting an erection when you really didn't want to, such as when you were dancing with a girl or walking into your aunt Mary's house for Thanksgiving dinner! But don't worry. Chances are nobody even noticed. And if they did, so what? Spontaneous erections usually go away after a few seconds anyway, so just take a few deep, calming breaths and trust that as you get older, your penis won't always misbehave.

> A quick note on hygiene <

Make sure you wash your private parts each time you shower, especially if you're not circumcised. The last thing you want is an infection or funky smell down there.

Should I do my own laundry? Some guys start to feel really weird about wanting to dump their sheets in the hamper more often than usual when they start having wet dreams. If it makes you feel less weird about it, learn how to use the washing machine and start to wash your sheets yourself. If anyone asks you about it, just say "I wanted to wear my Beastie Boys shirt so I just threw some other stuff in with it. No big deal." They probably won't ask you again.

3 <<< The Female of the Species >>>

As your body matures during puberty, your feelings toward girls are going to mature, too. For starters, you might find that you don't mind having them around as much as you used to. They don't seem like such pests anymore. And then there may be one or two you suddenly decide you actually kind of like. You might even start feeling kind of mushy about one of them. Maybe you'll even fall in love with her.

Sounds simple, right? You probably already know that it's not.

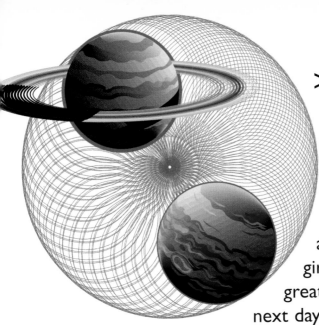

>> I Like Her . . . But She's Whacked! <<

During puberty, you may feel that girls are from another planet. One day a girl might act as if you're the greatest thing on earth, and the next day it's as though she wants nothing to do with you. It can be really, really confusing. The only way to explain this is that girls are going through just as many changes as you are. For everyone, moodiness comes with the territory. Chances are she occasionally thinks you're whacked, too.

>> What's Going On? <<

Like you, when girls go through puberty they undergo physical changes. Their hips are widening, which will help them to give birth to children when they're older. Like you, they are growing underarm hair and pubic hair. And they're also going to start menstruating—if they haven't already. That means that each month their bodies will produce an egg in the ovaries. The egg will travel through the fallopian tubes to the uterus. The woman's body will build up extra tissue and send lots of blood to the uterus to cushion the egg in

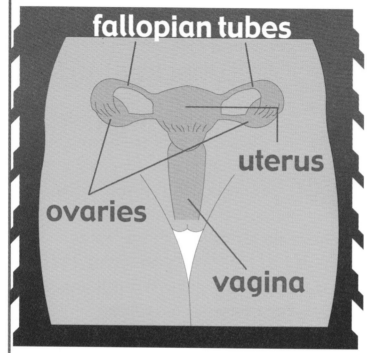

fallopian tubes

uterus

ovaries

vagina

case it's fertilized by a man's sperm and then grows into a baby. But an egg can wait around only so long.

So if that egg isn't fertilized, it will be flushed out through the woman's vagina— an opening between her legs—along with some tissue and blood, every month. Girls use pads or tampons to absorb the flow.

The vagina is also the opening that babies are born through. It is part of the vulva, which also includes the labia, folds of skin between a woman's legs that are sometimes referred to as lips. The labia surround the clitoris, which is designed to give women pleasure when touched. The urethra, the opening through which women urinate, is also part of the vulva.

>> Whoa! You're Losing Me with All These Fancy Names! <<

That's okay. Just know that now, like you, girls have a lot of new hormones running around their developing bodies. Like you, they'll have mood swings and confused emotions. So if a girl completely freaks out on you for some reason—maybe just for looking at her the wrong way—try to be understanding.

>> So How Do I Deal? <<

The best way to relate to girls is simply to be honest with them about how you feel. If there's someone you like, try to get to know her better. Maybe something romantic will grow out of it, maybe not. But at the very least, you will have gotten to know someone new, maybe made a new friend, and you will have practiced talking to a girl. Sometimes it does seem as if it requires Herculean courage just to have a conversation with one, right? Especially when they smell so nice, and when they do that thing where they flip their hair, and when they . . . well, that kind of leads us into the next chapter.

<<< Gettin' Jiggy with It >>>

>> Masturbation, Fantasies, and the Mechanics of Sex <<

There's a lot of bad information about sex floating around out there. Sure, all that biology stuff is pretty cut-and-dried. But when we move away from the pure scientific facts of what's happening to you, people—namely parents and teachers—get weird, and some of them just don't want to talk about it. You may feel weird asking questions, too, because you don't want people to think you're dumb or perverted. But if you feel that you can talk to your parents or an older brother or guidance counselor, go ahead and do it. Otherwise, keep on doing exactly what you're doing—reading. There are tons of ideas and opinions about sex out there (not all of them could possibly fit in this book!), and you need to figure out for yourself how you feel about certain things. Like, for example . . .

>> Masturbation <<

It's a proven fact that people touch their genitals from an early age. But most parents will tell their kids to stop or smack their hands away when they're young. A lot of people grow up feeling guilty about touching themselves. There are, of course, people who believe that masturbation—touching oneself for pleasure—is a sin, but the majority of people see it as part of a healthy, sexual life. And yes, girls do it too!

True or False?

If I masturbate too often, I'll run out of sperm before I'm old enough to have kids.

False: Your body is capable of producing millions and millions of sperm—more than you could ever use up. In fact, many of them get absorbed into your body when they're not used and new, fresher sperm are produced.

And for the record, masturbation won't make you blind or give you acne or have any other negative physical effects on your body.

Picture Perfect . . . NOT!

A lot of guys get turned on just looking at pictures of beautiful women—naked or not. This is totally natural, but it's also important to know that the girls you know—the girls you're going to date and be in relationships with—are different from the women in magazines. For starters, they're people you know—people who have thoughts, and opinions, and feelings that you're going to have to be sensitive to. Hot poster girls make for great fantasies, but they're no substitute for a real relationship with a real girl—even if it's not a sexual relationship.

>> It Takes Two <<

Okay, so what about when there's somebody else involved? Sex with another person is much more complicated than masturbation. First, there's another body to deal with. That means another brain, filled with tons of thoughts, fears, and emotions. Second, there are lots of risks, like disease. (More on that later.) But these are the basics of what happens between a man and woman who decide to have sex.

> One thing leads to another . . . <

Most sexual encounters begin with kissing, which can lead to other kinds of touching and caressing, called foreplay or petting. Foreplay is very pleasurable and fun; it's basically

just exploring each other's bodies—including the penis, testicles, breasts, and vulva. Foreplay also serves a purpose in a biological sense. For starters, it will give you an erection. For women, it triggers a number of bodily responses that prepare them for the possibility of sexual intercourse, during which the penis is inserted into the woman's vagina.

Once foreplay has begun, for example, the woman's body will start to produce fluids that serve as a lubricant to allow for penetration by the man's penis. The walls of her vagina will soften so they can expand as needed. In addition, parts of a woman's body, like the labia and clitoris, will become extra sensitive to touch.

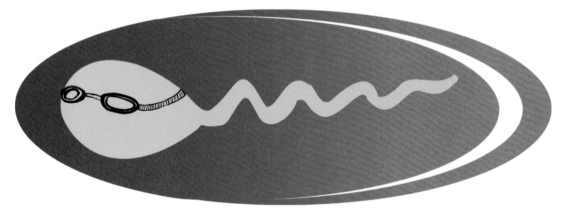

> . . . and sometimes that leads to an orgasm. <

The friction (two things rubbing together) that intercourse creates (friction can also be created by hand during masturbation or foreplay) can stimulate the man's penis to the

Q&A

Q: Okay, so a guy has an orgasm when he ejaculates. Do girls have orgasms?
A: Yes, women have orgasms, too. An orgasm happens inside her body, signaled by contractions in and around the walls of the uterus and vagina. For both males and females, an orgasm brings a feeling of urgency and release.

point where he will ejaculate inside the woman's vagina. Since sperm can swim their little hearts out—since their very purpose is to find an egg and fertilize it—condoms and other types of contraception are incredibly important during sex.

So there you go. That's what you wanted to know, right? Now everything's perfectly clear, right?

Wrong.

Knowing how sex is all supposed to work (kind of) doesn't solve all your problems. You're curious, but you're a little scared, too. And you want to grow up, but you also want to stay young. It's certainly not an easy time.

5 <<< Lust, Lies, and Locker Rooms >>>

PTTT!

Let's get one thing straight. Nobody likes stripping in front of friends, classmates, coaches, teammates, or teachers—especially not during puberty. Guys who have chest or armpit hair will feel self-conscious about it, and those who don't will too. Basically, nobody wins.

>> If I Look at Other Guys, Does That Mean I'm Gay? <<

You may feel as though you're a pervert if you try to sneak a peek at another guy. Almost every guy does this during puberty, so don't get all freaked out. It's normal to want to know what other bodies look like. The question of your sexuality—whether you're attracted to women or men—is different. It's a much more complex part of your identity that almost everyone questions during the teen years. So if you're not sure yet whether you're attracted to guys, girls, or both, don't worry. What matters is staying open to your true feelings.

>> Kiss and Tell <<

Sometimes locker rooms—or any place where there are no girls around, like all-boys' schools—become places where guys feel the need to brag about how far they've gone sexually. However, just because someone's talking about what he has done doesn't mean he has actually done it—or that he feels good about it if he did. A lot of people feel as if they have to pretend to be more experienced than they are in order to fit in. Sometimes you may feel that way, too. But don't believe everything you hear. Just do what's right for you. Let things happen naturally.

After I made out with Katie, I kind of lied to some of the guys and made it seem like we did more than we really did. I didn't exactly say what, but I let them think whatever they wanted. Somehow it got back to Katie, and everyone ended up knowing that I'd lied about it. I felt like more of a loser than I would have if I'd just told the truth. Because the truth—just kissing—was pretty great. But now Katie barely talks to me. I really screwed up.   —Matt, 16

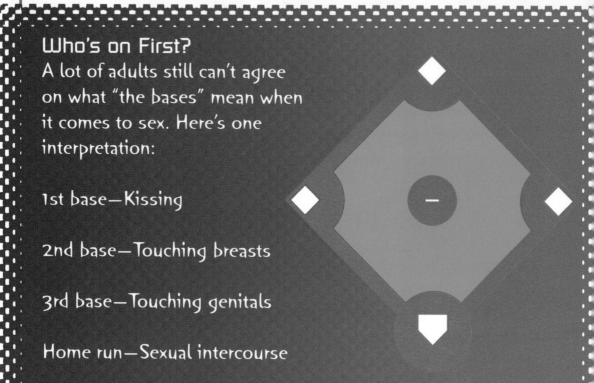

Who's on First?
A lot of adults still can't agree on what "the bases" mean when it comes to sex. Here's one interpretation:

1st base—Kissing

2nd base—Touching breasts

3rd base—Touching genitals

Home run—Sexual intercourse

>> Do Girls Think About "It" As Much As We Do? <<

During puberty, girls' fantasies are usually less sexually explicit and more romantic than boys'. This pretty much explains the popularity of "chick flicks." You do have some things in common, though. Like you, girls are worried about fitting in, and they get insecure if they think the rest of their friends are developing faster than they are.

Physical development aside, girls also worry about the choices they make regarding sex. They worry that they'll be seen as prudish if they don't get physical with guys. At the same time, they fear that they'll be seen as sluts if they do. In your own way, maybe you worry about those things, too.

It's okay, you can admit it. Guys are allowed to be sensitive these days. I swear.

<<< Check Your Head >>>

We've talked a lot in this book about what's happening to your body physically and what it's going to be capable of when you completely mature to adulthood in your late teens. What we haven't talked about so much is that all these new hormones swimming through your bloodstream are affecting your brain and your emotions.

You might suddenly develop a short temper. You might get upset more easily—by things that wouldn't have bothered you before. You'll probably feel a lot of emotions—like love and hate, fear and jealousy—more strongly than before. And sometimes even the slightest setback or insult will make you feel as though it's the end of the world.

Learn to be patient with yourself and with others. Right about now you'll probably be feeling like everyone except your best friends is the enemy. This may be super-true of your parents. But things will calm down.

Private! Keep Out!

If your parents don't think twice about walking into your bedroom without knocking, maybe it's time for a little role reversal: Sit them down and have a little talk with them. Explain that as you're growing up, you'd like them to respect your privacy the way you do theirs. Then make sure that you respect theirs.

Because you're feeling stronger emotions and stronger physical desires, it's important to use your brain during puberty. Use it to remind yourself that a pimple isn't the end of the world. Use it to keep your mouth shut when you're tempted to tell a tall tale. Use it to remind yourself that there are a lot of good reasons to postpone having sex.

> You could get hurt. <

Yes, sex is a physical act, but we're not talking about pulling a muscle here. Sex is a very powerful experience, and there are a lot of emotions involved when you get that close to someone else. When you take your clothes off with someone, you make yourself vulnerable. If you choose to become sexually involved with someone who doesn't feel the same way about you as you do about him or her, you could get hurt. When you do finally decide to have sex, choose your partner wisely.

> You could hurt somebody else.<

If you have sex with someone just for the sake of having sex, you might get more than you bargained for. It's possible that person will think it meant a lot more to you than it did. You'll only end up hurting that person and having to deal with a lot of bad feelings.

> Babies. <

Although your body may technically be ready to produce sperm and make a baby with a girl, actually being ready to father a child is

something else entirely. Today you need an education to get ahead in life. So you need to stay in school—and that's pretty hard to do when you're pushing around a stroller and carrying a diaper bag. The best time to have a kid is when you're an established adult with a job and a home of your own.

Yes, condoms and other forms of contraception are designed to prevent pregnancy, but they're not 100-percent guaranteed. Abstinence (not having sex) is the only surefire way to prevent pregnancy.

> You could contract HIV or other sexually transmitted diseases. <

HIV, a virus that can enter your bloodstream during sex, causes AIDS, a disease that attacks the human immune system. That's the part of your body that fights off germs. It's no joke that AIDS can kill you. It's true that many people who contract the HIV virus are living longer today with new medications, but they have to take tons of pills, and there's no guarantee.

In addition, other diseases, such as herpes or genital warts, can make your life a lot more complicated. Yes, there's such a thing as "safe sex," which means using a condom during intercourse. But condoms, which can break, are not guaranteed 100 percent. The safest sex really is no sex.

Five very serious reasons not to have sex:

Your values: If you believe that you shouldn't have sex until you're married or very much in love and committed, you should wait.

Your life: You could contract the HIV virus, which causes AIDS, which is life-threatening.

Your health: You could contract a number of other sexually trans-mitted diseases.

Your future: You could get a girl pregnant.

Your heart: You might not yet be prepared for the powerful feelings sex often causes.

Five not-so-serious reasons not to have sex:

It's illegal, depending on where you do it, whom you do it with, and how old both of you are.

You have nowhere to do it comfortably.

The big game is on.

Your parents would kill you.

Two words: Sony PlayStation.

>> Like a Virgin? <<

Today more and more men are deciding to put off sex. So although television and movies make it seem as if men have sex just to have sex, that's just not true of all men. It doesn't have to be true for you.

> I had sex when I was thirteen with a girl who lives on my block. I guess I kind of pressured her. We had no idea what we were doing and it really hurt for her. She started crying and I wanted to cry, too. I think it'll be a while before I try it again, and then with someone I really care about. Honestly, it scared me half to death. —Joe, 14

Everyone has different feelings about their own virginity. Some people don't want to lose it until they're married, or in love, or just older, or in a serious relationship. Whatever your feelings on the subject, the bottom line is that there really is no hurry.

When, in the future, you are truly ready to have sex, remember this: Never ever pressure a girl into having sex with you, or doing anything she doesn't want to do, and never lie to her (for example, tell her that you love her) in order to get what you want.

Now go back and read that last sentence again.

And now read it one more time.

Okay, now you can turn the page.

7 <<< Everything's Going to Be Just Fine. Really. >>>

After all this talk about how your entire body is changing, how your entire life is changing, and how you're suddenly becoming more of an adult with adult feelings and responsibilities, it may seem stupid to say "Don't worry about it." But here goes . . .

Don't worry about it. Really.

This is a confusing time, but it's also an exciting one. As you get older, more and more opportunities will open up for you. That's why it's important not to let this puberty/testosterone/sex thing get the best of you. There's school to finish. There's college. There's your career. There's life.

And all this romantic stuff? It'll all get easier with time and practice. When it feels right for you to have sex, you'll know it. In the meantime, you'll probably kiss a couple people. You'll probably make a few mistakes, have your feelings trampled on, trample on somebody else's feelings, and maybe fall in and out of love—a bunch of times.

Right now, your new sexual self might seem like all you want to think about. But do yourself a favor . . . don't

Things to Do Instead of Having Sex (That Will Make You Sexier When You're Older)

Exercise or play sports to stay fit.

Learn how to shoot pool. (A lot of people think it's sexy.)

Read poetry. (You can write love poems.)

Get a job. (You'll have money to go on dates.)

Volunteer for an organization that helps people in need. (It'll put your own life and worries in perspective.)

let it take over your life. Get involved in all sorts of stuff now. Participate in sports or activities you like. Make good friends of both genders. Get to know yourself. And as corny as it sounds, just have fun. There will come a time when you'll look back on all of this and laugh. So, if you can, try and laugh a little bit about it now, too.

<<< What's the Word? >>>

abortion   A medical procedure in which a pregnancy is terminated.

circumcision   A medical procedure in which the foreskin covering the shaft of the penis is cut away.

clitoris   Part of a woman's vulva, created to provide sexual pleasure when touched.

condom   A sleeve made of latex that slides over the penis to prevent the spread of disease and to block sperm.

contraception   Devices like condoms, or birth control pills, meant to prevent pregnancy.

ejaculation   The act of releasing semen through the penis.

erection   When the penis is in an aroused or hardened state, standing erect.

fertilization   The process that occurs when a male sperm penetrates a woman's egg, triggering the start of development of a new life.

foreplay   Kissing, caressing, and other activities that usually come before sexual intercourse.

genitals   Sex organs; in men, the penis and testicles; in women, the labia, clitoris, and vagina.

hormone   A product of living cells in the body that circulates in bodily fluids and produces a specific effect on cells somewhere else in the body.

intercourse   The act in which a man's penis is inserted into a woman's vagina.

42

masturbation The act of pleasuring oneself sexually by touch.

menstruation The monthly process by which blood and tissue are discharged or released from the uterus through the vagina.

nocturnal emissions Also known as wet dreams, when a man ejaculates, or releases semen, in his sleep.

orgasm The climax of sexual excitement, usually occurring toward the end of a sexual encounter and resulting in ejaculation (for men) and involuntary muscle contractions.

puberty The period during which someone first becomes capable of reproducing sexually; marked by maturing of the genitals, development of secondary sex characteristics (like pubic hair), and menstruation (in females).

pubic hair A secondary sex characteristic. Hair that grows on or around the genitals of a man or woman.

semen The white fluid that contains sperm.

sperm The male cell capable of fertilizing a woman's egg; carried in semen.

spontaneous erection An erection that happens without sexual stimulation of any kind, frequently during puberty.

testicles The testes and the scrotum, taken together.

testosterone The hormone responsible for triggering and maintaining secondary sex characteristics in men.

vagina The canal that opens between a woman's legs and leads to the uterus.

virginity The state of not having experienced sex.

vulva The female genitals, including the labia, clitoris, and vagina.

<<< For More Information >>>

If you have access to the Internet, check out these sites for more info:

Ask Doctor Marla
http://web.wwa.com/~docmarla
e-mail: docmarla@wwa.com

KidsHealth.org
http://kidshealth.org

PlannedParenthood (includes magazine, *Teenwire,* on teen sexual health)
http://www.plannedparenthood.org

React.com (on-line zine)
http://www.react.com

Virtual Kid's Puberty 101
http://www.virtualkid.com/sitemap.shtml

<<< For Further Reading >>>

Bourgeois, Paulette, Martin Wolfish, and Kim Martyn. *Changes in You and Me: A Book About Puberty, Mostly for Boys.* New York: Andrews McMeel Publishing, 1994.

Editors of Planet Dexter. *A Boy's Guide to Life: The Complete Instructions Written by Kids, for Kids.* Reading, MA: Addison Wesley Longman, 1997.

Graeville, Karen, Nick Castro, and Chava Castro. *What's Going On Down There: Questions Boys Find Hard to Ask.* New York: Walker & Co., 1999.

Madaras, Lynda. *The What's Happening to My Body? Book for Boys.* New York: Newmarket Press, 1988.

Martin, Karin A. *Puberty, Sexuality, and the Self: Boys and Girls at Adolescence.* New York: Routledge, 1996.

McCoy, Kathy, and Charles Wibbelsman. *Life Happens: A Guide to Friends, Failure, Sexuality, Love, Rejection, Addiction, Peer Pressure, Families, Loss, Depression, Change, and Other Challenges of Living.* New York: Putnam Berkley, 1996.

Roehm, Michelle, ed. *Boys Know It All: Wise Thoughts and Wacky Ideas from Guys Like You*. Hillsboro, OR: Beyond Words Publishing, 1998.

Sommers, Michael A. *Everything You Need to Know About Looking and Feeling Your Best: A Guide for Guys*. New York: Rosen Publishing Group, 1999.

<<< Index >>>

<<< Credits >>>

About the Author
Bill Kelly is a freelance writer who lives in Brooklyn, NY.

Photo Credits
All photos by Thaddeus Harden

Series Design and Layout
Oliver H. Rosenberg